I0664036

HOW
SHALL WE
LIVE?

because there is
a monk in all of us

Joan Chittister, OSB

Benetvision

$14.00
Item #B081

Quantity discounts available.

355 East Ninth Street
Erie, PA 16503-1107

Phone: 814-459-5994   Fax: 814-459-8066
benetvision@benetvision.org
www.benetvision.org

*Benetvision: Research and Resources
for Contemporary Spirituality*
is a ministry of the Benedictine Sisters of Erie.

Copyright 2006

No part of this publication may be reproduced in any manner
without prior permission of the publisher.

ISBN: 1-890890-19-7

06 07 08 09 5 4 3 2 1

Table of Contents

Introduction 7

A Spirituality
for the 21st Century 11

An Ancient Model
for Today 19

A Tradition
That Transforms 27

Creative Work 35

Holy Leisure 43

Stewardship 51

Community 59

Humility 67

Peace 75

Credits 82

Introduction

In early times,
those seeking to live a spiritual life
went and sought spiritual direction
from seasoned desert monastics saying,
"Abba...Amma, give me a word."

These insights or reflections
revolved around the values or visions of life
that the spiritual director thought most meaningful
for seekers at the present time.

In *How Shall We Live*
Joan Chittister looks to one of those spiritual masters,
Saint Benedict of Nursia for a "word"
that will illuminate our "darkening but beautiful world."
She seeks the "word" from two sources:
The *Rule of Saint Benedict* and
the *Life and Miracles of Saint Benedict*,
as recorded by a disciple, Pope Gregory the Great.

For over 1500 years the *Rule of Benedict* has guided
ordinary men and women in their search for God.
Joan Chittister probes the *Rule*
for six vital values that speak to a world
in political, economic and cultural turmoil:

work, holy leisure, stewardship, community, humility and peace.
With creative insight and deep wisdom she then explores six stories
from the *Life and Miracles of Saint Benedict*
that mirror these same values.

What "word" on creative work will help us define it
beyond money, power and security?
What "word" on holy leisure will return
balance to frenzied lives gone askew?
What "word" on stewardship will enable us to see
pollution, global warming, and waste as spiritual questions?
What "word" on community will give us a global vision?
What "word" on humility will force us to see beyond
our own wants and self-importance?
What "word" on peace will lead us
to be gentle with ourselves, with the earth and with the other?

The "word" from Benedict on these values
is complemented by stories and sayings from monastic lore
that have been tried by time and tradition.

Chittister subtitled this book, "because there is a monk in all of us."
And isn't it true? Isn't each of us a solitary seeker of God?
Isn't there a pounding desire in all of us
to break with the familiar and secure and leap into the unknown,
no matter the cost?
Don't all of us yearn to live a life that makes a difference?
Don't all of us set out on a journey
pressing to our hearts the burning question:
How shall we live?
In these times of chaos and confusion,
don't all of us come on bended knee and plead,
"Abba...Amma, give us a word."

—Mary Lou Kownacki, OSB

On the *Rule of Benedict*

Benedict of Nursia was born in the year 480. As a student in Rome, he tired of the decadent culture around him and left to live a simple spiritual life as a hermit in the countryside of Subiaco about thirty miles outside the city. It wasn't long, however, before he was discovered both by the people in the area and disciples who were themselves looking for a more meaningful way of life. Eventually he became founding abbot of a series of monasteries and founder of a way of life that was written down as *The Rule of Benedict.* Out of these associations sprang the monastic life that would eventually cover Europe. In our own day there are over 1400 communities of Benedictine and Cistercian men and women who live under this Rule. In addition to the professed monastics who follow the Benedictine way of life, there are innumerable laypersons around the globe who also find in the *Rule* a guide and a ground for their own lives in the middle of a chaotic and challenging world.

Benedict had a sister, Scholastica, who also dedicated her life to the pursuit of God. She, too, founded monasteries and became an abbatial figure. What is equally clear is that the brother and sister were emotionally close and a spiritual influence on one another till the time of her death.

On the *Dialogues of Gregory*

A follower of Benedict who became Pope Saint Gregory the Great preserved the life of Saint Benedict in a document called the *Dialogues of Gregory.* The *Dialogues* are the only source of biographical material that we have on either Benedict or Scholastica. Through stories in the metaphorical style of the time, the *Dialogues* give insight into the qualities and character of both of them rather than simple historical detail. The stories are fanciful to modern ears, perhaps, but logical to the heart. These are the things of which humanity is made: the spiritual life and human community. As a result, Benedict and Scholastica do not shine in the human constellation of stars because of who they are as individuals. No, Benedict and Scholastica stand out in history because of what their lives did for centuries of lives to follow them.

It is my belief that the way of life established by Benedict over 1500 years ago is a gift to our times, a beacon in the dark showing us *How To Live.*

Joan Chittister, OSB

9

A Spirituality
for the 21st Century

· ·

Reflection

There are two stories–one from the Sufi masters and one from the monastics of the desert–that may tell us most about what it means to live an illuminated life in hard times.

In the first, the Sufi tell about a spiritual elder who asked the disciples to name what was most important in life: wisdom or action? The disciples were unanimous in their opinions: "It's action, of course," they said. "After all, of what use is wisdom that does not show itself in action?" "Well, perhaps," the master said, "but of what use is action that proceeds from an unenlightened heart?"

In the second story from the desert monastics, Abba Poemen says of Abba John that he had prayed to God to take his passions away from him so that he might become free from care. "And, in fact," Abba John reported to him, "I now find myself in total peace, without an enemy." But Abba Poemen said to him, "Really? Well, in that case, go and beg God to stir up warfare within you again, for it is by warfare that the soul makes progress." And after that when warfare came Abba John no longer prayed that it might be taken away. Now he simply prayed: "Lord, give me the strength for the fight."

We may well learn from these ancients. It is a moment again in human history that needs deep wisdom and requires holy struggle. The map of the world is changing. People are starving to death on the television screens in our family rooms. People who have worked hard all their lives fear for their retirement while we continue to put more money into the cost of militarism and instruments of destruction in this society than we do into programs for human development.

What is the spirituality we need for the 21st Century? We face a choice: to retire from this fray into some paradise of marshmallow pieties where we can massage away the heat of the day, the questions of the time, the injustice of the age with spiritual nosegays and hypnotic exercises and protests of powerlessness–where we can live like pious moles in the heart of a twisted world and call that travesty "peace" and "religion." Or we can gather our strength for the struggle it will take to bring the reign of God now.

Where can we possibly go for a model of how to live in a world where we are being forced to choose between impossibles: between the impossibility of ignoring what is and the impossibility of accepting what is–and doing either of them in the name of God? My suggestion is that we stop drawing our sense of human possibility from the periods of exploration and their destruction of native peoples, or from the period of industrialization and its displacement of people, or from the periods of the world wars and their extermination of peoples. No, my suggestion is that little people–people like you and me–begin to look again to the fifth century and to the spiritual imagination and wondrous wisdom that made it new.

A Spirituality for the 21st Century

from the Life and Miracles of Benedict

Time to Think

This story from the *Dialogues* is a hard, a cruel one. It is also an important one. It is a scenario that happens too often in too many lives in too many ways. It is a drama that is too often the death of the spirit when it is really meant, perhaps, to release untapped life within us.

In this story, Benedict is prevailed upon, despite much reluctance and only after much persuasion, to become the abbot of a monastery that is failing and leaderless. Clearly, the group had lost its way and had deteriorated. Benedict, the monks realized, had the vision and spirit it would take to save the place. So they convinced him to leave his cave at Subiaco and go with them. It was a potentially great enterprise, this preservation of a monastery, and clearly worth his efforts, his interest and the redesign of his own life's agenda. He went.

When the community realized what it would demand from each of them to really revive the place, to take it to the heights of its own ideals, they balked. And, to stop the difficult and hated process,

When Benedict left the monastery that resented his efforts to renew them, he simply went back to being who he was before he went there. It is a very liberating model. After all, it is what we are when there is nothing else in life that is the real gauge of a person's quality. It is the willingness to stand alone that tests our mettle.

✠

Benedict didn't coax, cajole and compromise with the group on the grounds that change was slow and patience was more important than truth. He unmasked the evil and left the place. Have you ever disclaimed a group because of its basic dishonesty? What happened to you as a result?

13

they set out to kill this respected and effective abbot by poisoning his table wine. The vessel broke when he blessed it and he realized immediately what had happened. "You didn't have to do this," he said to the community. "You could just have asked me to leave."

And then the *Dialogues* give us the key to the story: "He left that place and went back to live alone with himself."

The implications of the story are far too clear. Not to confront evil—as Benedict did—is an evil in itself. It is not possible to save a thing from itself. Like the monks in the story, we must realize that in order to change, we must want to change. The important thing in life is to have a center so sound that nothing outside ourselves can disturb it.

✠

"Non-cooperation with evil is as much a duty as is cooperation with good," Gandhi wrote. The question is, of course, why was there not one single monk who resisted the plot against Benedict? And then there is the question even worse than that: What evil is there that I myself have never resisted? Never sent a postcard about it to a politician; never said a word at a cocktail party; never raised a single question in a church group on that behalf. No wonder the world is in the situation it is.

✠

Benedict made it clear that the desire for good is no excuse for the exercise of evil in its behalf. To become what we hate—as mean as the killers, as obsessed as the haters—is neither the goal nor the greatness of the spiritual life.

A Spirituality for the 21st Century
Rule of Benedict

Never lose hope in God's mercy.

Rule of Benedict 4.74

A Spirituality for the 21st Century
Monastic Wisdom

Amma Syncletica said:
"In the beginning,
there is struggle and a lot of work
for those who come near to God.
But after that,
there is indescribable joy.
It is just like building a fire:
at first it's smoky and your eyes water,
but later you get the desired result.
Thus we ought
to light the divine fire in ourselves
with tears and effort."

Desert Sayings

Give Us A Word

Abba Poemen said about Abba Pior
that every single day
he made a fresh beginning.

Desert Sayings

We go from beginning to beginning,
by beginnings that have no end.

Gregory of Nyssa, *VIIIth Homily on the Song*

See what no eye can see,
go where no foot can go,
choose that which is no choice—
then you may hear what makes no sound—
God's voice.

Angelus Silesius

Do not seek enlightenment
unless you seek it
as a person whose hair is on fire
seeks a pond.

Sri Ramakrishna

A Spirituality for the 21st Century

How Shall We Live?

"...begin to look again to the fifth century
and to the spiritual imagination
and wondrous wisdom
that made it new."

Joan Chittister, OSB

An Ancient Model for Today

· ·

Reflection

In fifth century Europe, Rome, the superpower then, was declining and the world was a restless, seething, fearsome place. The church itself was more temporal power than spiritual leader. With the breakdown of the Roman government, the Roman highway system was unguarded. Pirating and pillaging and looting were commonplace. No one was safe. Barbarians were crashing with a vengeance through once-tight borders. Slavery, the exploitation of one set of human beings by another for the sake of the one at the expense of the other, was a given.

The western world was awash with the defenseless poor. Their lands were gone; their governments were in chaos. Families and tribes and cities were fractured everywhere.

Rome itself had been sacked by vandals. Force had become a substitute for government. Power had become the drug of choice. All of society's little people were ground up, ground down, ground to dust by the competition for it.

There was no institution big enough to confront this chaos; no system mighty enough to bring calm to this storm. Why?

Because the very people who were oppressed by it, appalled by it, or destroyed by it supported it. The very people who had the most to gain by its reform sustained it. How? Simply by assuming that nothing else was possible and nothing could be done. Simply by accepting the idea that circumstances were unchangeable and that what was, should be: "Well, that's the way life is," the realists said. "This is still the best of all possible worlds," politicians said. "There's nothing we can do about it," the masses said. Indeed, some people always accept or approve or surrender to the system. But not all. Not everyone.

In the fifth century, one person, a young man, resolved to change the system not by confronting it, but by eroding its credibility. He simply decided to change people's opinions about what life had to be by himself living otherwise, by refusing to accept the moral standards around him, by forming people into organized communities, by outlawing slavery where he was, by the sharing of goods, by caring for the earth, by teaching a new perspective on our place in the universe. And because of his example, thousands more did the same. Thousands more, in villages, capitals, and cities all over Europe, did the same.

The young man was Benedict of Nursia whom we now call "saint" when what we really mean is hero, icon, model, star–Christian. For over 1500 years now, popes across the centuries have called Benedict of Nursia "The Patron of Europe" and accredited the Benedictine lifestyle that he developed in the darkest periods of western history with the very preservation of European culture.

The values he modeled maintained the social order, safeguarded learning, gave refuge to travelers and made rules for war that brought peace to chaos. Those values transformed Europe into a garden again and modeled the equality of peoples and provided a link between heaven and earth.

An Ancient Model for Today

from the Life and Miracles of Benedict

Time to Think

This story from the *Dialogues* of *Gregory* is a simple but familiar one to people everywhere. It is about love and difficulties, about people's needs and people's circumstances, about desires in conflict. It's a story we all live every day of our lives.

By the time this incident takes place, Gregory tells us, Benedict has already started three monasteries: all of them flourishing, all of them at the top of the mountain, all of them far from the waters of the river below. It was a wonderful place for a monastic retreat but it was hard living for the monastics there. They had to walk the mountains every day of the year—under the blistering sun and in the dangerous rain and despite the biting wind and through the hot, thick undergrowth carrying pails of water for cooking and cleaning and personal needs. As far as the monastics were concerned, they explained to Abbot Benedict, it was time to move the monasteries.

Benedict listened but under no condition did he want to move. This was the right place to be. This was the right way to live. There was nothing to be gained by starting over, by moving down the mountain closer to the river and away from where they could concentrate on what they were doing in peace. What's worse, there was a great

There are two life lessons that take some people the greater part of a lifetime to learn. The first demands that I discover who I am—what I, myself, really want in life and what I need to give in life if I am ever to be whole. The second lies in giving myself permission to be myself no matter who tries to persuade me to be otherwise. Have you managed to learn either one of these lessons completely yet?

✝

The problem with love is that we expect it to last without tending to it. We do better than that with radishes.

21

deal to lose if they did. Something had to be done to bring both visions together.

That night Benedict went to the top of the mountain with the boy Placid, prayed over a spot, marked it with three stones and the next day directed the monastics to dig there for water. "If you dig down a little, you will see that almighty God has the power to bring forth water even from that rocky summit and in His goodness relieve you of the hardship of such a hard climb," Benedict told them. "To this day," the *Dialogues* read, "a stream still flows from that place–down to the ravine below."

It's an important story for all of us who are struggling to make our lives and our relationships fit. It helps us to remember the basics.

In order to make anything better we have to be willing to unearth the issues that surround it. We have to go deeper into the problem. We need to explore the center of the self. We have to discover what we need in order to enable everyone to endure what cannot be changed, to create what must be provided, to make the impossible possible, to distinguish the circumstances from the essence of a thing. We must not allow incidentals to obstruct the essence of our lives.

✠

"The true opposite of love is not hate but indifference," Joseph Fletcher wrote. It would have been so easy for Benedict simply not to care whether the monastics liked the situation as it was or not. He could simply have said, "This is monastic life, take it or leave it." "This is what my work demands, take it or leave it." "This is what I want, take it or leave it." "This is what I'm going to do, take it or leave it." But he didn't. Love listens. Love negotiates. Love satisfies.

✠

There is one holy goal in life: to refuse to make life more difficult for others than it already is. Then, if I can truly do that, the difficulties of my own life can only disappear.

An Ancient Model for Today
Rule of Benedict

Listen and bend the ear
of your heart.

Rule of Benedict, Prologue 1

An Ancient Model for Today
Monastic Wisdom

An old man was bitter
and challenged Jacob with a complaint.
"All my life I have searched for meaning,"
he said. "The meaning is in the search,"
said Jacob, waving off the man's distress.
"Then I will never find the meaning?"
"No," said Jacob.
"You will never stop looking."
Jacob held his voice for a moment,
unsure if he had been too harsh.
"My friend," Jacob began again,
"know you are a man with a lantern
who goes in search of a light."

Noah ben Shea
from *Jacob the Baker*

An Ancient Model for Today

Give Us A Word

Amma Sarah said:
"If I pray to God that all people
might be inspired because of me,
I would find myself repenting at the door of every house.
I would rather pray that my heart
be pure toward everybody."

Desert Sayings

The place you are right now
God circled on a map for you.

Hafiz

Whenever I'm feeling discouraged
I vow with all beings
to remember how Ling-yun
saw peach trees bloom
after thirty long years.

Robert Aitken Roshi

How far are you from me, O Fruit?
I am hidden in your heart, O Flower.

Rabindranath Tagore

An Ancient Model for Today

How Shall We Live?

"...begin to look again to the fifth century
and to the spiritual imagination
and wondrous wisdom
that made it new."

Joan Chittister, OSB

A Tradition
That Transforms

. . . .

Reflection
_____

The Benedictine model was successful but questions remain. How was this transformation achieved and what does it have to do with us at this moment in history? The answer, I suggest, lies in realizing that what does not live in us cannot thrive in our society.

Benedict demanded a great deal more than the practice of private religious exercises which, good as they are, necessary as they are, always run the risk of bringing more personal comfort than they do spiritual growth.

Benedict modeled a way of walking through the world that made the whole world a better place. If the twenty-first century needs anything at all it may well be a return to the life-giving vision of Benedict the Illuminated One. Perhaps we need a new reverence for bold Benedictine wisdom if civilization is to be saved again–and this time the very planet preserved.

The reality is that our world has knowledge and technology aplenty but lacks wisdom and spirituality. The reality is that our world is locked into one value system and is dry to the core for want of another. We are taught to want money, to retire at the earliest possible age, to get ahead whatever the cost to others, to win at any cost, at all costs, to worship at the altar of the self, and to be in control of everything, always.

But those values are a recipe for extinction, a blueprint for human destruction. They are precisely the values that have destroyed the rain forests and melted the polar ice cap and left peasant farmers without land. These values have left babies of color dead in their mothers' bony arms, old women to sleep in public parks, and one out of five preschool children in the United States in poverty. In the richest nation in the world, 20 million are hungry and 40 million have no health insurance.

The values that saved western Europe in a social climate akin to our own were creative work, not profit-making; holy leisure, not personal escapism; wise stewardship, not exploitation; loving community, not individualism raised to the level of the pathological; humility, not arrogant superiority; and a commitment to peace, not domination. Today, just as 1,500 years ago, those values have been foresworn. We dearly need them again.

A Tradition That Transforms

from the Life and Miracles of Benedict

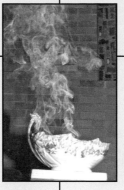

Time to Think

By the time this incident happened Benedict was already an abbot of some renown. His sister, Scholastica—many say his twin—had been "consecrated to God since her youth" and was herself a person of repute.

During one of their annual visits, Scholastica, inspired by the depth of their conversation, asked Benedict to remain overnight in the place where they were meeting in order to continue their talk and reflection on spiritual things. Benedict wouldn't even think of it. It was getting dark; it was time to get back to the monastery; it was time to get on with the regular routine of the spiritual life. Scholastica, the *Dialogues* say, put her head down on the table in deep prayer. Suddenly, out of nowhere, a great storm brought with it flash floods and Benedict realized that he could not possibly return to the monastery that night. And the *Dialogues* say, "he complained bitterly." He said, "God forgive you, sister! What have you done?" Scholastica answered simply, "I asked you for a favor and you refused. I asked my God and I got it."

Have you ever reflected on the laws of the land deeply enough to see if they could possibly square with a conscience formed on love? Segregation, for instance, or capital punishment or abortion or even war? Benedict was concerned with the laws of the institution. Scholastica leaves us with a model of the laws of love. Which do you choose in these situations?

✠

It isn't easy to allow ourselves to be human once we have set out to be holy. That's why so few of us get to be truly holy. We suppress what we are instead of sanctifying it. What is there in yourself that you fear to face and therefore fail to turn to positive energy?

29

The story is a vein worth mining for a lifetime.

She was intent on pursuing the values of the life, not simply its rules. She wanted to think about the values the rules were meant to develop in us. She was on a higher level of law than he was.

It was one thing to keep a schedule, a regulation, a law, a custom but it was also necessary to break them at times.

When the rules stopped black people from getting the same quality education as white people, it was time to lift the rules.

When the rules stop women from earning the same amount of money for the same kind of work as men do, it is time to change the rules.

When the rules allow western companies to pay white workers one wage and non-western workers another, it is time to reevaluate the rules.

We make rules to suit our own needs while they destroy others and we call them "the will of God."

The reexamination of the rules is a necessary, a constant, part of the spiritual life.

✠

A woman has as much power in the eyes of God as any man and we must recognize women, too, as spiritual guides.

✠

Scholastica saw life in a new way when she wanted Benedict to forget the demands of the day for awhile. Benedict saw life differently when he saw Scholastica draw on the power of God. We all need to see the link between the daily and the divine in our lives or else we shall separate the very elements that are necessary to our own full development, a commitment to the commonplace and a sensitivity to the cosmic in which we dwell.

A Tradition That Transforms
Rule of Benedict

Let us open our eyes to the light that comes from God
and our ears to the voice from heaven
that every day calls out this charge:
"If today you hear God's voice, do not harden your hearts."
(Ps. 94:8).

Rule of Benedict, Prologue 9

A Tradition That Transforms
Monastic Wisdom

Abba Lot went to see Abba Joseph and said:
"Abba, as much as I am able
I practice a small rule, a little fasting,
some prayer and meditation,
and remain quiet, and as much as possible
I keep my thoughts clean.
What else should I do?"
Then the old man stood up
and stretched out his hands toward heaven,
and his fingers became like ten torches of flame.
And he said:
"If you wish, you can become fire."

Desert Sayings

A Tradition That Transforms

Give Us A Word

___

And everything comes to One
As we dance on, dance on, dance on.

Theodore Roethke

Say *Yes* when nobody asked.

Lao Proverb

An elder said:
"Let us acquire the main virtue,
love.
Fasting is nothing,
late nights are nothing,
and labor is nothing,
if love is not there.
Indeed it is written:
God is love."

Desert Sayings

I never knew
how to worship
until I knew how to love.

Henry Ward Beecher

A Tradition That Transforms

How Shall We Live?

"...begin to look again to the fifth century
and to the spiritual imagination
and wondrous wisdom
that made it new."

Joan Chittister, OSB

Creative Work

. . . .

Reflection

There are two poles pulling at the modern concept of work. At one pole is the workaholic. At the other pole sits the pseudo-contemplative. Workaholics work because they have learned that what they do is the only value they have. Or they work because they want to avoid having to do anything else in life like family or prayer or living. Or they work because they really don't want to work at all. What they really want is money, money, money.

Pseudo-contemplatives, on the other hand, want to spend their hours gazing into space or reflecting. They spend every new year of life processing last year's. Pseudo-contemplatives have missed the point completely that Adam and Eve were put in the garden in order "to till it and to keep it," not to gaze at it; not to live off of it; not to lounge around it. They were put there to co-create it!

In the fifth century, the young visionary Benedict addressed the need for both work and contemplation. He required specified periods for manual labor, prayer and prayerful reading. Benedict was not about saccharine piety and theological niceties. He set out to save the world by putting work and meditation on the same level.

To Benedict, work was always to be done with the vision in mind. Laziness and irresponsibility, oppression and exploitation, obsessive, neurotic, insane production of the goods of destruction in peacetime and the ravishment of the globe are, then, to the Benedictine mind, all forms of injustice and thievery because they set out to tear the world down rather than to build it up.

Work is our gift to the world. It is work that ties us to the rest of humankind and binds us to the future. It is work that saves us from total self-centeredness and leads to self-fulfillment. It lets us give back as much as we take from life.

But the work of this century has become, at least for us, what we call security. Annual defense spending by the United States is three times the combined annual defense spending of Russia, China, Cuba, Iran, Iraq, Libya, North Korea, Sudan and Syria. So infected have science and industry become by the allure of inflated military contracts that we doggedly, patriotically, and immorally resist the loss of the military-industrial symbiosis for fear that the country would be economically damaged. But the simplest arithmetic would tell us that spending a billion dollars on the production of guided missiles creates about 9,000 jobs. If we spent the same amount of money on pollution control, however, it would create 16,000 jobs. A billion dollars on local transit would create 21,000 jobs; and a billion dollars on educational services would create 63,000 jobs. According to Employment Research Associates, $40 billion invested in a conversion program could bring a net gain of more than 650,000 jobs.

If we had the wisdom of Benedict, if we had a spirituality of creative work, we could do it.

The goal of life is not to get out of working. The goal of life is to work and work and work because the world is unfinished and it is our responsibility to keep building and creating.

36

Creative Work

from the Life and Miracles of Benedict

When the young man Benedict abandoned his studies and fled the grossness of metropolitan Rome to go into solitude, he was accompanied only by his old nurse. In one village where they stayed, the nurse borrowed a special tray to prepare a meal. But then, inadvertently, she dropped the tray and broke it. It was a matter to be taken seriously in a place and time where neither mass production nor money were common. The old woman wept. Benedict, the *Dialogues* say, knelt down, took the two parts of the broken plate into his hands, and weeping himself, prayed. No sooner had he finished praying than he noticed that the tray was mended and, with great joy, returned it to his nurse.

It is a simple little story, almost laughable to the scientific, rationalistic types of our time. Yet is tells us something too long lost, it seems, under layers of data and levels of systems.

It tells us that we must honor the laborers of our society—hear their struggles, attend to their needs, protect their jobs and

The story of Benedict is a call to take the plight of the poor seriously. The question of our time is, Is it possible to live a truly spiritual life unless we care about the things that the poor care about.

✠

Elie Wiesel has written: "When someone suffers and it is not you, they come first." Benedict had a personal agenda that he allowed to be interrupted by an upset old nurse. Whose cry have you permitted to interrupt your life today?

✠

We must be menders of what is broken in society, not its judges, not its mocking observers.

37

assure their security. It tells us we must value honest work at all levels of society.

It tells us that there is nothing so small that it does not deserve our attention. It tells us that we must weep with those who weep. It tells us that the lives of the little ones of the world depend on us. It tells us that every living being has a right to dignity, protection and help. It tells us that we must be menders of what is broken.

✠

An African proverb reads: "Not to aid one in distress is to kill them in your heart." Clearly what is argued here is the responsibility that each of us has to the dignity of the other. Singleness is not enough. Only love is the measure of goodness.

Creative Work
Rule of Benedict

First of all, every time you begin a good work,
you must pray to God most earnestly
to bring it to perfection.

Rule of Benedict, Prologue 4

Creative Work
Monastic Wisdom

It was said about one brother that when he
had woven baskets and put handles on them,
he heard a monk next door saying: "What shall
I do? The trader is coming but I don't have the
handles to put on my baskets!" Then he took the
handles off his own baskets and brought them
to his neighbor, saying: "Look, I have these left
over. Why don't you put them on your baskets?"
And he made his brother's work complete, as
there was need, leaving his own unfinished.

Desert Sayings

Give Us A Word

Among the maidens grieving at the death of Macrina,
were those who had been left prostrate along the roadways
at the time of the famine. Macrina had picked them up,
nursed them, brought them back to health
and then became their teacher and guide.

Life of Saint Macrina by Gregory, bishop of Nyssa

An old man said:
"I never wanted work that was useful to me
but loss to my brother.
For I have this expectation,
that which helps my brother is fruitful for me."

Desert Sayings

Do you want a test to know if your work in life is over?
If you are alive, it isn't.

Richard Bach

Once upon a time, the ancients tell us,
a disciple said to the rabbi, "God took six days
to create the world and it is not perfect.
How is that possible?"
"Could you have done better?" the rabbi asked.
"Yes, I think I could have," the disciple said.
"Then what are you waiting for?" the rabbi said.
"Go ahead. Start working."

Hasidic Tale

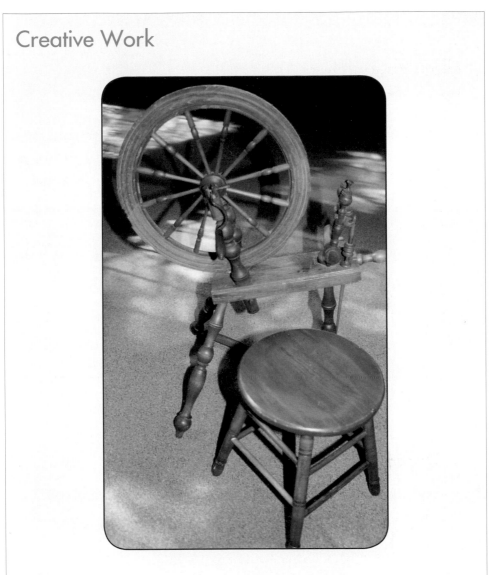

How Shall We Live?

"...begin to look again to the fifth century
and to the spiritual imagination
and wondrous wisdom
that made it new."

Joan Chittister, OSB

Holy
Leisure

. . . .

Reflection
_____

Leisure is as essential to Benedictine spirituality as is work. But real leisure, holy leisure, Sabbath leisure has more to do with quality of life than it does with play and vacations. The rabbis taught that the purpose of leisure was threefold: first, to free the poor as well as the rich for at least one day a week. Nobody had to take an order from anybody on the Sabbath. The second purpose was to give people time to evaluate their work as God had evaluated the work of creation, to see if their work was life-giving. Finally, the purpose of Sabbath leisure was to give people time to contemplate the real meaning of life.

If anything has brought the modern world to the brink of destruction it must surely be the loss of Sabbath. The purpose of holy leisure is to bring lives gone askew back into balance, to allow time for a contemplative as well as a productive life. It is holy leisure that brings us to ask what it is to follow the gospel in this situation now, in this place here. When people sleep in metro stations, it is holy leisure that asks, Why? When during the first Iraqi war, 200,000 soldiers and another 100,000 civilians–most of them children–are exterminated in 43 days and their land made desolate, it is holy leisure that asks how such a thing can possibly be of God if we are truly a Christian and civilized people. In the second Iraqi war, a reporter asked a high-ranking official why there are no estimates reported of the number of Iraqi dead. The answer was, "That is a number in which I have no interest whatsoever." It is holy leisure that breaks the secular silence and asks a Sabbath question, Why don't you?

When our environmental rape, air pollution, deforestation and toxic wastes result in famine, desertification, and poverty around the globe for people who had nothing to do with the doing of it...it is holy leisure that asks how it was that our today became more important than God's tomorrow.

Holy leisure is the foundation of contemplation and contemplation is the ability to see the world as God sees the world. Indeed, the contemplative life will not be destroyed by activity, but by the absence of contemplation.

In Benedictine spirituality life is not divided into parts, one holy and the other mundane. To the Benedictine mind all of life is holy. All of life's actions bear the scrutiny of all of life's ideals. All of life is to be held in anointed hands.

Holy Leisure

from the Life and Miracles of Benedict

Time to Think

The young Benedict felt smothered with public attention as the pressure on him increased by the day, distracting him in his attempt to live a calm and centered spiritual life. He knew he had to find a space more suitable for a serious and reflective life. So, he went to a cave.

Cave dwelling was not an especially unusual kind of retreat for intensely spiritual persons of the time. It's not surprising then that Romanus, a monk from a nearby monastery, was deeply impressed with the sincerity of Benedict's spiritual search. To mark the legitimacy of that intensity, the old monk clothed Benedict in the style established at the time for religious figures and supported him in his pursuit of the spiritual life. He lowered food down the side of the mountain to him. He guarded Benedict's sanctuary by telling no one of his presence in the area. Most of all, he took care of Benedict at great inconvenience to himself. The food he brought Benedict came from his own plate and he left his monastery to care for him without even asking his abbot

The philosopher Blaise Pascal wrote: "The unhappiness of a person resides in one thing–to be unable to remain peacefully in a room." It is silence and solitude that bring us face to face with ourselves and the inner wars we must win if we are ever to become truly whole. Stay in a room alone for an hour and make a list of things you think about during that time. Which one of those things are you avoiding?

☩

Solitude and loneliness are not the same thing. Loneliness is the sign that something is lacking. The purpose of solitude is to bring us home to the center of ourselves with such serenity that we could lose everything and, in the end, lose nothing of the fullness

45

for permission to do so.

Without Romanus, Benedict could not have lived the life he did; without Benedict, perhaps Romanus would never have known the fullness of his own.

The lessons for us and our time are many. We all need space and time away from the pressures of our successes. Silence is an important part of thought. A talent for solitude is a measure of a person's self development. What we nurture in life is what we are and what we give the world.

of life at all. When you are alone are you lonely or are you in solitude? If loneliness is what it's about, what you may need most is the cultivation of the richness of solitude.

✝

Like Benedict, everybody has to have a cave—a place and a time to take care of themselves before their talents devour them. What's your cave? When were you in it last? For how long?

✝

The monk, Romanus, who provided food for Benedict in the cave knew that there were some things in life that deserve to be nourished simply for their own sake. Art is one, music is another, good reading is a third; but the power of the contemplative vision is the greatest of them all. Thanks to the support of Romanus, Benedict became visionary to the centuries. What are you helping to preserve for the next generation?

Holy Leisure
Rule of Benedict

Listen readily
to holy reading,
and devote yourself
often to prayer.

Rule of Benedict 4.55-56

Holy Leisure
Monastic Wisdom

On one occasion, some brothers had visited Abba Arsenius,
a former Roman noble and model of austerity, and the
pleasant Abba Moses, an Ethiopian and former robber.
Arsenius remained absorbed in his prayer, and said nothing
to the visitors. Abba Moses, on the other hand received them
with joy and sent them back after having given them heartfelt
hospitality. One of the Fathers came to hear of this, and
made this prayer: "God, please explain to me why one of
them shuns humans, because of your name, while the other
welcomes them with open arms, because of your name."
Then, in a dream, he saw two boats sailing side by side,
on the river. In one, he saw Abba Arsenius, in contemplation
with the Spirit of God. In the other, Abba Moses was with the
angels of God, who served him honey cakes.

Desert Sayings

Holy Leisure
Give Us A Word

A brother went to see Abba Moses
and begged him for a word.
And the old man said:
"Go and sit in your cell, and your cell will teach you everything."

Desert Sayings

At our best, we become Sabbath for one another.
We are the emptiness, the day of rest.
We become space, that our loved ones,
the lost and sorrowful, may find rest in us.

Wayne Muller in *Sabbath*

The training of the imagination implies a certain freedom
and this freedom implies a certain capacity to choose
and to find its own appropriate nourishment.
Thus in the interior life there should be moments
of relaxation, freedom and "browsing."
Perhaps the best way to do this is in the midst of nature,
but also in literature.
Perhaps also a certain amount of art is necessary and music.

Thomas Merton, *Contemplation in a World of Action*

In the city of Brahman, there is a dwelling
in the form of a lotus flower,
and within it, there is an inner space.
One should search for that which is within that inner space.
It is this we must seek.
It is this that we should desire to know.

Maitri Upanishad 6:28

Holy Leisure

How Shall We Live?

"...begin to look again to the fifth century
and to the spiritual imagination
and wondrous wisdom
that made it new."

Joan Chittister, OSB

Stewardship

· ·

Reflection

If mindfulness of the sacred in life is what holds life together it is the lack of awareness and lack of sacred care, and lack of holy stewardship that is fraying it. We have covered the earth with concrete. In 20 years Chicago used up 46 per cent more land mass in mini-malls while the population grew only 4 per cent. And we wonder why children have little respect for the land.

We spill industrial and residential refuse into our rivers and wonder why boaters drop their paper plates and plastic bags and old rubber shoes overboard. We pump pollution into our skies and question the rising incidence of lung cancer and of childhood asthma. We produce items that do not decay and package things in containers that cannot be recycled. We fill our foods with preservatives that poison the human body and wonder why we're not feeling well.

We make earth and heaven one large refuse dump, a running sore of humanity, and wonder why whole species of animals are becoming extinct and forests have died and the ozone shield has shriveled. The hole in the ozone has increased 37 per cent since

1997 and now exceeds the size of North America. We have failed to steward the land and the sea and the air and we see none of these as moral questions, though we go to church and we go to church, and we go to church.

In Africa and Bangladesh, drought is destroying food supplies for years to come. But every time we use a spray can that emits a toxin contributing to global warming, you and I contribute in our own small way to that drought. Stewardship demands that we begin to reverse these trends. The world's poor are suffering and it is we who are creating that suffering for so many who cry out to us for help.

The U.S. produces 163 metric tons of garbage a year–401 pounds of garbage per U. S. citizen, starting with me. Much of what the world cannot dispose of is made up of the styrofoam cups we use and the tin cans we discard rather than recycle. Meanwhile, the rest of the world reuses three to five times as much material as we do. In the same way, what we spray on our gardens and inject into our animals ruins human health around the world.

If we are to be a spiritual people, a holy people, we have to consider how to take these concerns into our own lives so that others can live safely. If I would not serve poisoned food to those I love, then, because I have internalized Benedictine spirituality, I will write postcards to legislators asking them to see that our food production processes do not poison others. I'll support the local food bank or soup kitchen to see that the hungry are fed. I'll join a group interested in ecology. I'll send money I earn to groups that are working to make the world a better place for everyone.

Benedictine spirituality, the spirituality that brought the world back from the edge before, asks us to spend our time well, to contemplate the divine in the human, to treat everything in the world as sacred. No, exploitation has not saved us. We need the wisdom of stewardship now.

Stewardship

from the Life and Miracles of Benedict

Time to Think

Benedictine spirituality is not made of marshmallow and clouds. If anything, the *Dialogues* and their presentation of Benedict of Nursia dispel with great clarity the image of stargazing monastics rapt in reflection and unaware of the world. This definition of contemplation makes life a foreign object; living, an enemy to spirituality. The *Dialogues*, on the other hand, link contemplation and action with astonishing vigor.

In this story the world intrudes on the monastery with awful directness. It is a time of crop failures, famine, and social breakdown. The poor, caught on arid land, are keenly affected. With no goods to barter, no harvest to sell, no staples to sustain them, honest and hardworking people are reduced to begging. It is a painful time, even for those of social station.

One of them, the sub-deacon Agapitus, reduced to desperation apparently, turns to Benedict's monastery for help. And Benedict, overcome with pity, orders the monastery's business manager or cellarer to give him the very last vial of the

Life's major problem does not lie in choosing good from evil. That's obvious and easy. No, life's real problem comes in choosing good from good. What's the answer? That's also easy: When values are in conflict, always choose the higher one.

✠

We cringe at the thought of Benedict's anger. He threw the vial of oil right out the window. Are saints supposed to do those things? Well, as Templeton said: "If we had been holier people, we would have been angrier oftener." What is going on in the world that you should be developing some anger about if the world is ever going to be a better place to live?

53

monastery's oil, a staple and necessity of the day. But the cellarer, an efficient and sensible man, aware of the impact that action could have on the monastery itself, did not do it. When Benedict, a charismatic visionary, realized what had happened, he became very angry. He called the cellarer to his room, took the vial of oil out of his hands and, in the sight of the entire monastic community, ordered another monk to throw the vial out the monastery window. Then, point made, Benedict had the unbroken vial brought back and given to Agapitus. He rebuked the cellarer in front of the community, knelt down and began to pray. Suddenly, an empty oil-cask in the room began to fill with oil, overflowed the rim and covered the floor.

It is a stark and shocking scene and it says a great deal to our times. It says there are values beyond security and good sense. It says everything we have belongs to the poor. It says the challenge of leadership is to lead us to live beyond ourselves. It says that those who give to others will be filled themselves with whatever things they need.

✛

The world is filled with churchgoers and the world is filled with the obscenely poor. Go figure.

✛

Why was Benedict so angry? Because the monastery had been given a chance to be generous and failed the test? No, because the monastery had been given a chance to love dangerously and had opted to be safe instead. Have you ever loved dangerously? What happened to you as a result?

Stewardship
Rule of Benedict

As soon as anyone knocks,
or a poor person calls out, the porter replies,
"Thanks be to God" or "Your blessing, please";
then, with all the gentleness that comes
from the fear of God,
the porter provides a prompt answer
with the warmth of love.

Rule of Benedict 66.3–4

Stewardship
Monastic Wisdom

There are three stages in one's spiritual development, the elder taught, "the carnal, the spiritual and the divine." The eager disciple asked, "What is the carnal stage?" "That's the stage when trees are seen as trees and mountains as mountains," the elder answered. "And the spiritual?" the disciple continued. "The spiritual is when one looks more deeply into things. Then trees are no longer trees and mountains are no longer mountains." "And the divine?" the disciple asked in awe. "Ah, yes, the divine," the Elder smiled. "Well, divine enlightenment is when trees become trees again and mountains, mountains."

Zen Story

Stewardship
Give Us A Word

Every time you pick up a piece of trash along the road,
say to yourself, "Holy, Holy, Holy is the house of God."

Edward Hays

May it be beautiful
before you
behind you
above you
below you
may beauty surround you.

Navajo chant

Sacred One, teach us love, compassion and honor,
that we may heal the earth.

Ojibway prayer

The world is truly a holy place.
Venite adoremus. Come let us adore.

Teilhard de Chardin

Stewardship

How Shall We Live?

"...begin to look again to the fifth century
and to the spiritual imagination
and wondrous wisdom
that made it new."

Joan Chittister, OSB

Community

....

_____

We exist to be miracle workers to one another. It is in community that we are called to grow. It is in community that we come to see God in the other. It is in community that we see our own emptiness filled up. It is community that calls me beyond the pinched horizons of my own life, my own country, my own race, and gives me the gifts I do not have within me. But Americans, you and I, have been groomed for independence and self-sufficiency, not community.

So prevailing is the syndrome that in our lifetimes–for the first time in mental health history–narcissism, an inordinate and insulating love of self, has been added to the DSM-3 handbook of mental health illnesses in this country. Narcissism has become a hallmark of American culture. The idea that we, above all the others of the world, are unique and superior and normative and entitled to expect endless resources and cheap energy and high wages here, thanks to slave wages there, has become a signature of the American Dream. It is also a sin against human community.

The function of community is to enable us to be about something greater than ourselves. Today's culture tells us that we ourselves are enough to be concerned about and that, if we do that, everything else will take care of itself. I take care of me, you take care of you, that's going to be good for everybody. But that kind of unenlightened altruism has brought us the deterioration of the centers of our own cities while the suburbs flourished, brought us the greatest corporate greed the world has ever known and it has brought us a sense of human alienation that has corroded our neighborhoods, our children, our culture and the very core of American life.

In a world without a sense of human community all of life becomes a television screen–remote, unreal and unreachable–while we sit in the fortresses we call our homes–small, isolated and insular–and fear anyone we don't know, be it the Arabs and Chinese, the gays and the blacks, while life goes by and we have missed its real richness in the others we have not met.

A Benedictine spirituality of community calls for more than togetherness. Togetherness is very cheap community. A Benedictine spirituality of community calls for the open mind and the open heart.

Benedict called for minds open to the shattering implications of the scriptures. Jesus was an assault on every closed mind in Israel. To those who thought that illness was punishment for sin, Jesus called for openness. To those who considered tax collectors incapable of salvation, Jesus called for openness. To those who believed that the messiah had to be a military figure to be real, Jesus was a call to openness. Benedict also calls us to open heartedness.

The Benedictine heart–the heart that saved Europe before us–is a place without boundaries, a place where the truth of the oneness of the human community shatters all barriers and opens all doors, refuses all prejudices, welcomes all strangers, listens to all voices, black and white, Arab and Jew, male and female.

The data is in. The world is an electronic, commercial, political village. We cannot, you and I, go on much longer simply nodding to neighbors in the name of hospitality and community. We must begin to see the immorality of being socially, globally unconscious and narcissistic and calling it the free market and the free world.

Community

from the Life and Miracles of Benedict

Time to Think

The biographer Gregory tells us that Benedict sent the young man Placid to fetch water. Impatient, maybe, or just inexperienced, Placid let the bucket fill too rapidly, lost his balance and was pulled into the lake, where the current quickly seized him and carried him from shore. When Benedict realized what had happened, he ordered another young monk, Maurus, to go to Placid's rescue. But first, Gregory is careful to relate, Maurus begged Benedict for a blessing. Then Maurus rushed down the mountain, ran straight across the surface of the water to where Placid was flailing for his life and dragged him back to safety, amazed himself at what he had done.

The story is an important one for friends and disciples alike. It gives us layers and layers of life to think about. Like Maurus, it is unlikely that most of us would have done anything of real significance in our lives if we had not been called to it by someone else.

Everyone needs a wisdom figure in life who gives direction, confidence and

Sometimes it happens: you simply meet someone who brings another piece of life to your soul like a missing corner of a jigsaw puzzle. That is not acquaintanceship. That is grace, something designed to provide presence when you consider yourself most alone, something meant to call us to grow in depth, self-understanding and the healing balm of self-revelation.

✠

Maurus did what he did for two reasons: first, because he had been called to it by someone wiser than himself and second, because it was worth doing. A call and a purpose are the axles on which life turns. Who has called you to life? In what are you involved that is life-giving to someone else?

spiritual guidance. Friendship calls us beyond ourselves to love without expecting return, to live without counting costs. Friendship is our ability to see the needs of the other. The miracles in our lives are seldom of our own making. They are simply the function of a few loving friends, the people around us who care enough to call us beyond our own definitions of ourselves. Indeed, love inspires.

✠

Perhaps the most interesting part of the Benedict story is that Placid went for the water alone, Benedict saw the accident when he was alone and Maurus was sent to the rescue alone. And yet, each of them needed one another in order to discover something new in themselves—abandonment, insight and courage. It is a vivid and vital demonstration of real love.

✠

"Wonder is the beginning of wisdom," a Greek proverb reminds us. Maybe, but we are far more prone to evaluate anything that is different from us instead of standing in awe of it. Imagine what could happen in the world if we stood in awe of African culture, in awe of strong women and gentle men, in awe of new ideas and new questions. Instead, we block them or reject them or fear them. Then we miss our chance to appreciate the whole world.

Community
Rule of Benedict

Let them prefer nothing whatever to Christ,
and may Christ bring us all together
to everlasting life.

Rule of Benedict 72.11

Community
Monastic Wisdom

One day Chau-chou fell down in the snow
and called out, "Help me up; help me up."
A monk came and lay down beside him.
Then Chau-chou got up and went away.

Zen Koan

Community
Give Us A Word

If you live alone, whose feet will you wash?

Saint Basil

One is not absolutely alone,
one cannot live and die for oneself alone.
My life and my death
are not purely and simply my own business.
I live by and for others, and my death involves others.

Thomas Merton, *Conjectures of a Guilty Bystander*

Ananda, the beloved disciple of the Buddha,
once asked his teacher and friend
about the place of friendship in the spiritual journey.
"Master, is friendship half of the spiritual life?" he asked.
The Enlightened One responded: "Nay, Ananda,
a friendship is the whole of the spiritual life."

Macrina persuaded our mother to renounce her usual mode
of life, her manners as a noble lady, and the services she
used to receive from her slaves. Thus she shared in the
common way of life of the virgins she had with her.
From the slaves and servants they had been,
she made them her sisters, living at the same level,
eating at the same table, using the same bedding,
adopting the same means of living:
all differences of rank were suppressed in their lives.

The Life of Macrina by Gregory of Nyssa

Community

How Shall We Live?

"...begin to look again to the fifth century
and to the spiritual imagination
and wondrous wisdom
that made it new."

Joan Chittister, OSB

Humility

. . . .

Reflection

Benedict makes the keystone value of his rule of life, a chapter on humility that was written for Roman men in a society that valued machoism, power and independence at least as much as ours does. It is humility, Benedict taught, that provides the basis for human community and a basis for union with God.

"The first degree of humility," the *Rule of Benedict* teaches, "is to keep the fear of God always before one's eyes." The implications are obvious: to live well in this world, we must steep ourselves in the mind of God. We must ask what God wants for the world rather than simply what we want for our private, personal selves.

We have bartered the future for the sake of the comfort of a few. But no peoples have the right to gobble up the world for their own sakes. We must all come again to fear God. We have made ourselves the gods of the twenty-first century to whom the rest of the world pays tribute, asking sacrifices from those least able to afford it.

Like the Incas, we, too, have stooped to immolating children–

Iraqi babies go on giving their lives every day in adoration of the "resolve" of the United States of America to crush what it wants to crush in the name of "saving" it. Yet even our own children lack food. I live in the inner city where our soup kitchen and pantry are the only lifeline for many of our neighbors: elderly women, sick men, educationally limited teenagers, America's permanent underclass. While our politicians compete for office on the size of their tax breaks for the wealthy, we abhor welfare for the poor in the form of food stamps, subsidized housing, and day care. Welfare for the rich that we call tax breaks, we applaud.

Like the Greeks and Romans we, too, continue to enslave peoples "for their own good." We require developing nations to spend less and less on schools and health and roads for their own people so that the poorest people in the world can pay the richest people in the world for debts that they have repaid in interest over and over and over again.

Like the ancient Chinese, western industries bind the feet of people all over the world–making it impossible for them to move ahead–by taking their resources and exploiting their laborers for the sake of the most prosperous people in the history of the world. And then say that what we give the poor is better than nothing. No doubt about it: there is great room for fear of God here.

The arrogance of those who make themselves the center of the universe is destroying our world: our technology has outstripped our souls. We need the wisdom of humility now. We need that quality of life that makes it possible for people to see beyond themselves, to value the other, to touch the world gently, peacefully and make it better as we go.

Humility

from the Life and Miracles of Benedict

This story from the *Dialogues* is about pretense.

Totila, King of the Goths (one of the Germanic tribes that breached the borders of the Roman empire when Rome was no longer strong enough militarily to maintain its boundaries against foreign immigrants), was a ruthless marauder. He was also a curious creature. He had heard about Benedict–the simple monk, yes, but also a prophet, leader and spiritual strong man of the time. The thought of making contact with him first hand was too fascinating an experience to miss. It was too much fun for Totila to even think of passing up. So, he made an appointment to see Abbot Benedict himself. To test Benedict's gift of prophecy, or to tease his troops, maybe, he sent his servant, Riggio, to the meeting disguised as himself. He could hear the stories over beer and beef already: "And there was Riggio, my horse guard, dressed like me! Ha! ha! And the great holy man bowed and scraped. Ha, ha! Some prophet, ha, ha! He never even knew the difference!"

Time to Think

Pretense freezes the soul. One of the most consistent of spiritual lessons from the ancient world, taught by spiritual guides long before psychology as a discipline even existed, is that in order to make progress as a human being we must each be thoroughly known by somebody. Self-exposure is key to growth. Is there anyone in the world with whom you are completely open? Completely?

✠

"I am as my Creator made me," Minnie Smith wrote, "and since my Creator is satisfied, so am I." Think of all the musicians who want to be linguists and all the welders who want to be woodworkers, and all

Except that he did.

When Riggio, dressed in fine garments and attended by servants approached him, Benedict looked at him quietly and said, "Son, take off those gowns. They do not belong to you." The laughing stopped. The meeting ended. Riggio was embarrassed. Totila was sobered to the core. We ourselves are left with a lot to think about. People see through us when we pretend to be what we are not. Wearing a mask does not make us what or who we are pretending to be. Being free to be ourselves is one of the great achievements of life. All the things in the world can't make us something we aren't.

the teachers who want to be writers. Poor souls. Imagine spending your whole life looking into a mirror, unsatisfied. Not only would that take a lot of time, but, it would also waste a lot of energy that could be used to make the world better.

✠

The story tells us that Benedict told Riggio to take off his dishonest robes; it doesn't say that Benedict showed less respect to Riggio when he was in peasant clothes or showed more respect to Totila when he was dressed in kingly robes. Are you as attentive to the garbage collector as you are to the local clergy? If not, aren't you precisely the reason that people dress up to fool us?

✠

Benedict saw right through Riggio and saved him from the empty life that is a pretender's fate. If you're lucky, someplace along the line someone has seen through you, too, and told you so. Who was it? What changed in you as a result?

Humility
Rule of Benedict

Having ascended
all these steps of humility,
the monk will soon arrive
at that perfect love of God
that casts out fear.

Rule of Benedict 7.67

Humility
Monastic Wisdom

I walked up to an old, old monk and asked him,
"What is the audacity of humility?"
This man had never met me before,
but do you know what his answer was?
"To be the first to say
'I love you.'"

from *Tales of a Magic Monastery* by Theophane the Monk

Humility
Give Us A Word

When people are proud,
they envy the accomplishments of others
and then stir up every kind of evil.

Hildegard of Bingen, *Book of Life's Merits*

Every human being
goes through a door to the kingdom of God.
This door is exactly as high as you are
when you walk on your knees.

Andrew Harvey

We come spinning out of nothingness,
scattering stars like dust.

Rumi

Amma Theodora said that a teacher
ought to be a stranger to the desire
for domination, vainglory, and pride.
A teacher should not be fooled by flattery,
nor be blinded by gifts, conquered by the stomach,
nor dominated by anger.
A teacher should be patient, gentle and humble
as far as possible; successfully tested
and without partisanship, full of concern,
and a lover of souls.

Desert Sayings

Humility

How Shall We Live?

"...begin to look again to the fifth century
and to the spiritual imagination
and wondrous wisdom
that made it new."

Joan Chittister, OSB

Peace

. . . .

Reflection

Benedictine spirituality is a spirituality consciously designed to disarm the heart, to soften the soul, to quiet the turmoil within. It is a vision of nonviolence in a world for which violence is the air we breathe, the songs we sing, the heroes we worship and the business we do. At one time, in this country, we could teach that wheat was our major export. Now we must teach that weapons are.

But we are called to better than that. Be soft with others, the *Rule* teaches, and you will have peace. Be simple in your needs and you will have peace. Be humble in what you demand of life and you will have peace. Be giving in what you take to life and you will have peace. Refuse to make war on the innocent others in order to vanquish your political enemies, and you will have peace. Stop the wars within yourself and you will have peace.

Peace comes from not allowing any part of us to control the rest of us. Peace depends on our being gentle with ourselves, gentle with the other, and gentle with the earth.

Imagine a world where small children are not jerked down supermarket aisles in the name of discipline. Imagine a world where it would be possible to watch television for one whole night on any station and not be subjected to shootouts, beatings, muggings and rapes in the name of entertainment.

Imagine a world where people could find good jobs without

having to be part of a war machine designed to destroy the earth in the name of defense. Imagine a world where other races and nations and peoples are not demonized to justify our militarism. But more important perhaps for now, imagine a home where members of the family do not shout at one another or slap one another into subjection or bully one another into compliance or intimidate one another into domestic slavery.

Imagine a home where being a little boy did not mean having to prove himself with his fists or his muscles or his willingness either to give or to take pain. Imagine a home where both its boys and its girls, its women and its men could cry. Imagine what life would be like if we ourselves forgave–really forgave, our families, our colleagues, our children, and our spouses. Imagine your own life centered around creative work, holy leisure, stewardship, community, humility and peace. Would your one life, my one life, make any difference?

Well, the rabbis teach that when Moses tapped the shore with his staff, the waters did not roll back. And when Moses tapped the water with his staff, nothing happened. But when the first Jew walked into the water, then the Red Sea parted and Israel was saved. The miracle of the Red Sea was not the parting of the water, but that the first Jew walked in. Only then did the others follow.

We can ignore and accept things as they are or we can choose to grapple with them. We can surrender to them or we can struggle to change them. We can run away from the call to contemplation or we can embrace it with both wisdom and action, taking our disintegrating world back again one heart at a time, starting with yours and mine. And we can, if we will, like Moses and Benedict and one solitary Jew at the edge of the Red Sea, take the first step to lead a people to new life.

In the face of profit and comfort, exploitation and narcissism, superiority and domination, let us beseech God for the wisdom to take action. Like the ancients before us, let us beg God, now and always, forever and everywhere, to stir up holy warfare in our souls so that we refuse to be either executioners or victims in a world rife with both oppressors and oppressed.

Let us resolve again to follow the fiery-eyed Benedict of Nursia whose one life illuminated the western world. Let us, in other words, live Benedictine spirituality and illuminate our own darkening but beautiful world.

Peace

from the Life and Miracles of Benedict

Of all the stories told about Benedict, this one may be the most impacting of all on our own lives. Most of us will never work miracles or found monasteries or humble invaders, that's for sure. But one thing we can all learn to do is to see. This story is about a special kind of seeing.

Benedict, the story tells, left the company of a neighboring abbot after an evening's conversation about the spiritual life. The period pre-dates both universities and books, remember, let alone televisions and radios. Personal conversation was the key to learning then—a factor that may well explain the popularity of gurus and spiritual masters in that culture. At any rate, people came in droves to talk to Benedict about their spiritual questions, the great no less than the simple.

On this particular night, it is the Abbot Severanus, a deeply prayerful person himself, with whom Benedict has been talking. But then, retiring to his own room, alone and filled with ideas on the spiritual life, Benedict suddenly began to see what he had never seen before: the sky filled

Time to Think

Remember that it was after they had been discussing spiritual things that Benedict's vision was enlarged to include the whole world. It takes a spiritual sensitivity to hold the whole globe and all its needs in our hearts. Any spirituality that makes our hearts narrower than the globe is a bogus spirituality for sure.

☩

We talk about contemplation as if it were some kind of spiritual magic. Actually, the contemplative is the person who is so immersed in the will of God that they come to see the whole world as God sees the world. The fact is that all of us are called to be contemplatives.

with light and, in the center of it, he saw a whirling globe—in a period in which no one had ever seen the globe at all. "Benedict saw the whole world as in a single ray of light," the *Dialogues* tell us. More than that, while he watched, Benedict saw the soul of his friend, Abbot Germanus, taken into heaven. Astounded by the sight and intent on testing his own perceptions, Benedict called on Abbot Severanus, a solid and dependable person, to look at the sky, and sent a monk to inquire about Germanus as well. The confirmation was clear: Severanus, too, saw the vision and Germanus, he learned, had indeed died at the very time. Benedict had developed sight and insight. Benedict had begun to see things differently.

The implications for us and our own lives abound. The spiritual life enlarges a person's vision. When we begin to see as God sees, we see far beyond ourselves. Contemplation is a very human thing.

✠

It was night when Benedict saw the vision of his life. That's what usually happens to us, too. Just when we think that light will never come into our lives again, we begin to see a whole new world around us.

✠

At first it seems to be a contradiction: at the very time that Benedict saw the whole world in one glance, he saw only one person in it. But once we begin to look at the world as God looks at the world, that's exactly what happens. We see every person in it as unique, precious, all-absorbing. People cease to be numbers and stereotypes and races and sexes. They become individuals to us. Every one of them on their twisted, limping way to God.

Peace
Rule of Benedict

Pray for your enemies out of love for Christ.
If you have a dispute with someone,
make peace with them
before the sun goes down.

Rule of Benedict 4.72-73

Peace
Monastic Wisdom

During the persecution of the Church under Maximin, Antony
gathered other monks and went to Alexandria to serve the
persecuted. In the law court, he showed great enthusiasm,
stirring to readiness those who were called forth as contestants,
and receiving them as they underwent martyrdom and remaining
in their company until they were perfected. When the judge saw
the fearlessness of Antony and of those with him, he issued the
order that none of the monks were to appear in the law court,
nor were they to stay in the city at all. All the others thought it
wise to go into hiding that day, but Antony took this so seriously
as to wash his upper garment and to stand the next day in a
prominent place in front, and to be clearly visible to the prefect.
When, while all marveled at this, the prefect, passing by with
his escort, saw him, he stood there calmly, demonstrating the
purposefulness that belongs to us Christians.

The Life of Antony by Athanasius

79

Peace
Give Us A Word

Be the change you wish to see in the world.

Gandhi

What then will you give us, Lord?
What are you going to give us?
"Peace I give you. My peace I leave for you,"
says the Lord. That is enough for me:
gratefully I accept what you leave,
and I let go of what you retain.
If it pleases you, I do not doubt that it is for my good.
I want peace, I desire peace, and nothing more.
If there is anyone unsatisfied with peace,
they will be unsatisfied with you.

Bernard of Clairvaux, on the *Song of Songs*.

In you, O Jesus, true peace,
may I have peace upon peace forever,
so that through you I may come to that peace
which surpasses all understanding,
where happily I may see you in yourself forever.
Amen.

Gertrude the Great, *Spiritual Exercises*

Acquire inward peace
and a multitude around you will be saved.

Saint Seraphim

How Shall We Live?

"...begin to look again to the fifth century
and to the spiritual imagination
and wondrous wisdom
that made it new."

Joan Chittister, OSB

Spirituality & Health magazine, Dec. 2003, printed an edited version of a talk by Joan Chittister at the 2003 Trinity Institute. The main text for this book used both the edited and unedited version of her address. We thank *Spirituality & Health* magazine for permission to use the title, *How Shall We Live?* www.spiritualityhealth.com

Photographers

Cover	Bernadette Sullivan, OSB
Page 10	Bernadette Sullivan, OSB
Page 18	Bernadette Sullivan, OSB
Page 26	Claire Hudert, OSB
Page 34	Mary Miller, OSB
Page 42	Julie Mohan and Adrienne Monestere, oblates
Page 50	Benetvision file photo
Page 58	Lucia Marie Surmik, OSB
Page 66	Mary Miller, OSB
Page 74	Lucia Marie Surmik, OSB